ALWYN COX

Dangerous Journey

GW00503635

MACMILLAN

Founding Editor: John Milne

The Macmillan Readers provide a choice of enjoyable reading materials for learners of English. The series is published at six levels – Starter, Beginner, Elementary, Pre-intermediate, Intermediate and Upper.

Level control

Information, structure and vocabulary are controlled to suit the students' ability at each level.

The number of words at each level:

Starter	about 300 basic words
Beginner	about 600 basic words
Elementary	about 1100 basic words
Pre-intermediate	about 1400 basic words
Intermediate	about 1600 basic words
Upper	about 2200 basic words

Vocabulary

Some difficult words and phrases in this book are important for understanding the story. Some of these words are explained in the story and some are shown in the pictures. From Pre-intermediate level upwards, words are marked with a number like this: …³. These words are explained in the Glossary at the end of the book.

There was forest all round. All round for hundreds of kilometres. And there were no roads in the forest. There were only tracks.

Two tents stood in a clearing. Two men were standing near the tents. The younger man, Manuel, was making coffee on a small stove. He looked up at the sky.

'It's going to rain today,' he said.

'1 know,' replied Leon. 'And the rain will turn the ground into mud. Then we'll never get back to base.'

Four men were working in the forest. They were looking for iron and other metals. Leon was the boss and he was angry.

It was early morning. Leon and Manuel were ready to leave. But Joe and Pedro were our in the forest.

'They left in the truck two days ago,' said Leon. 'They're very late.'

Joe was always making trouble. He was younger than Leon and he was clever. He wanted to be boss.

Manuel poured the coffee into mugs and the two men drank it slowly. Suddenly they heard the sound of a truck.

'They're back,' said Manuel.

The truck came up the rough track. It stopped near the tents. Joe jumped out. He was a big man with red hair. He was smiling. His smile made Leon more angry.

'You're late,' said Leon. 'Where have you been?'

'Hunting,' replied Joe. And he held up his rifle.

'Hunting,' Leon shouted angrily. 'That's not your job. We haven't time for hunting.'

'We were away for two days,' replied Joe. 'We're not very late.'

'I'm the boss here!' Leon shouted.

Joe looked at Leon angrily. He was not smiling now.

'We're late — very late,' said Leon. 'The rain will start soon and then there will be mud everywhere. We must leave now.

Manuel took down the tents and Joe and Pedro put the boxes into the truck.

5

'Hurry!' shouted Leon. 'It's ten o'clock. Let's go.'

Soon everything was in the truck. Joe sat in the driver's seat. Leon sat beside him. Manuel and Pedro climbed into the back of the truck.

Joe started the engine and the journey began. They drove easily for the first twenty kilometres. Then they came to a stream.

'There was no water here last week!' Pedro shouted to Manuel. 'Look at the water now.

The stream was full of water. Joe slowed down and drove the truck carefully through the rushing water.

They crossed the stream and Joe drove faster. The

rain was now falling heavily. The track was very muddy and the truck began to slide.

'Watch our!' shouted Leon. But it was too late.

The truck stopped. The wheels were still turning, but the truck was not moving. The wheels were turning round and round in the mud.

Leon got out and Pedro and Manuel jumped down. Joe sat in the driver s seat.

Leon looked at the wheels in the mud. Then he looked up at Joe.

'It's your fault,' he said angrily. 'You were driving too fast.'

'Pedro, you cut branches from those trees,' ordered
Leon. 'And you, Manuel, throw the branches under the
wheels.'

Pedro got a large knife out of the truck and Manuel
helped him.

Leon turned to Joe. 'You, come and help us.

Joe did not move. 'I'm driving the truck,' he said.
'That's my job.'

'I'm boss here!' shouted Leon. 'Come and help us.'

Joe did not say anything. He did not get out of the
truck. Leon looked at him angrily. Then Leon walked
away.

Manuel and Pedro threw branches under the wheels. 'OK. That's enough,' said Leon. 'Let's go.'

Joe started the engine again. Pedro and Manuel pushed the back of the truck. The wheels turned and the engine roared. But the truck did not move.

'Push harder,' shouted Leon.

Suddenly, the truck moved forward. It was out of the mud. Pedro and Manuel shouted happily.

At that moment, a large branch flew up from under a wheel. It hit Leon's arm. He stepped back and fell in the mud.

'Stop the truck!' shouted Manuel. 'Leon's hurt.'

10

At midday, it was still raining heavily. The track was covered with mud. Joe drove slowly and the truck did not stop again.

They climbed up a steep hill. On the other side, the track went down to a river. It was the biggest river in the forest. This was the last river between the men and their base. An old wooden bridge crossed over the river.

They drove down towards the bridge.

'Look!' Leon shouted to Joe. 'Something's wrong. It's the bridge. It's broken.'

Joe did not stop the truck. He drove down slowly to the bank of the river. He drove to the edge of the broken bridge. Then he stopped. They all got our of the truck. They stood in silence. Nobody spoke. They looked at the broken bridge and at the rushing water.

Pedro spoke first. 'There is no way across the river now. How can we get back to base?'

'We must get help,' said Leon. 'Pedro, you climb back up the hill. Take the radio with you and call base. Perhaps they'll hear you and send help.'

Manuel lifted the radio out of the truck and fixed it to Pedro's back.

Joe stopped them. 'It won't work,' he said.

'Why not?' asked Leon.

'It isn't a strong radio,' replied Joe. 'We're too far away from the base. No one will hear us from this side of the river. We must cross the river by ourselves.'

'We can't,' said Leon. 'We must get help.'

'We can't get help from here,' said Joe. 'We must cross the river first. Then we can get help.'

'But how do we get across?' asked Leon. 'It's too dangerous. Look at the water.

The rain was still falling heavily and the water was rising.

'I have a plan,' said Joe.

Leon looked at Joe and smiled.

'You're clever, Joe,' Leon said. 'You always have plans. But they never work!'

'Let's listen to Joe's plan,' said Manuel.

'We can use the boat,' said Joe.

Leon laughed. 'Don't be stupid. The boat's too small for four people. And look at the rushing water. It will carry the boat away.'

'But we've got a rope,' said Joe. 'We can tie the rope to the boat. With luck, the water will carry the boat to the other side.'

'We can try it,' said Pedro.

'It won't work,' said Leon.

'It will work,' said Joe. 'Look, I'll show you.'

'We tie a rope to this end of the bridge.'

'Then we tie the rope to the boat and carry it up the river.'

'Two of us get into the boat and push it into the river.'

'We paddle hard to get to the other side.'

'We tie the rope to the other end of the bridge.'

'One of us pulls the rope and brings the boat back.'

'it won't work,' Leon said. 'But we can try it.

'I'll go first,' Joe said. 'it's my plan.'

'No, let me go,' said Pedro. 'I am stronger.

'You can both go,' said Leon. 'Pedro, you stay on the other side. Joe, you bring the boat back and then you can take Manuel. Then you can come back again for me.'

'Good,' Joe said. 'Pedro, you bring the radio. You can use it on the other side of the river.

Pedro got the rubber boat out of the truck and pumped it up. Leon helped him with his right arm.

There was a long rope in the back of the truck. Joe tied it to the broken bridge. Manuel tied the other end of the rope to the rubber boat.

'It's a long rope,' Leon said. 'It'll be all right.'

'Hurry,' said Joe. 'The water is rising quickly.'

Joe and Pedro carried the boat. Manuel and Leon walked behind them.

Manuel held the boat. Joe and Pedro climbed in.

The rushing water took the boat into the middle of the river.

The boat crossed to the other side. It came near the bridge.

Joe held on. Pedro climbed out of the boat.

Pedro tied the rope to a piece of the bridge.

Pedro stayed on the far side of the river. Joe pulled hard on the rope and the boat slowly came back to Leon and Manuel.

'You get in now, Manuel,' said Leon. 'I'm going last.'

'No, you're not,' Manuel replied. 'Your arm is broken. You can't get into the boat alone. You need help. I'll help you.

'Manuel is right,' said Joe. 'You need help, Leon.'

Manuel helped Leon into the boat. He sat down in the boat and Joe pulled hard on the rope.

Trouble came suddenly. Joe and Leon were in the middle of the river. Leon saw the tree first. The rushing water was pulling it down the river.

'Look out!' Leon shouted.

Joe looked round. At that moment, the branches of the tree hit the boat. Joe held onto the rope. His feet slipped and the boat moved away from him.

'Hold onto the rope!' Leon shouted.

But Joe did not listen. He let go of the rope and swam towards the rubber boat.

Joe was a good swimmer and he soon reached the boat. He held it tightly and kicked his legs hard in the water. The boat moved away from the tree.

'Good,' Joe shouted to Leon. 'The boat's free.'

'Leave the boat!' shouted Leon. 'Save yourself.'

Joe did not listen. He held the boat and kicked his legs.

A few moments later, Joe heard a loud noise.

'What's that?' he asked Leon.

'It's a waterfall,' replied Leon. 'The water will pull the boat over. Leave the boat. Save yourself.'

'Look!' shouted Joe. 'There's a rock! In front of us. We must reach it.'

'Don't be a fool,' said Leon. 'Save yourself. You can't save me.

The water rushed round the boat. It was pulling them towards the waterfall. Joe kicked his legs harder. The boat moved quickly towards the rock.

'Get ready,' shouted Joe. 'Jump for the rock!'

Leon was ready.

The boat came near the rock and Leon jumped.

Joe let go of the boat and swam to the rock.

The two men lay on the rock. For a few minutes they did not say anything. Then Leon turned and smiled at Joe. Joe had saved his life.

'We're not safe yet,' Joe shouted. 'The rain has stopped but the water is still rising. It'll cover the rock in an hour or two.'

Joe was right. There was water all round the two men. In front of them, the water dropped over the waterfall. Behind them, there was the broken bridge.

'We must get help,' said Leon. 'But how?'

'Pedro,' replied Joe. 'He can help us. He's got the radio.'

Pedro was waiting on the far side of the river. He watched Joe and Leon. They climbed onto the rock. They were safe.

They won't be safe for long, thought Pedro. I must call base and get help.

Pedro climbed up the hill behind him. He walked quickly for half an hour. At the top of the hill, he climbed onto a high rock. He took the radio off his back and pulled our the aerial. Pedro spoke into the radio.

'PX75 calling base. PX75 calling base.'

He waited and listened.

'PX75 calling base. PX75 calling base.'

There was no reply.

'PX75 calling base. PX75 calling base.'

Philip was sitting at the control desk. He was listening to the radio. PX75 was Leon's number. Philip turned the dials of the radio. The voice became clearer.

'Hello, PX75,' said Philip. 'This is base. What's your message? Over.'

'Hello, base. PX75 here. Pedro speaking. Can you hear me?'

'Loud and clear, Pedro. What's your message? Over.'

'We're in trouble,' said Pedro. 'The bridge over the River Sandano is broken. Joe and Leon are on a rock in the middle of the river. They are above the waterfall. Can you send help? Over.'

'River Sandano. Near bridge. Above waterfall. OK Pedro. Help is coming. Over.

Pedro climbed down the hill to the broken bridge. Manuel was waiting on the other side of the river. Pedro shouted and Manuel waved.

Both men looked down the river. The water was rising fast and the rock looked very small now.

On the rock, Joe was holding Leon in his arms. Leon's arm was covered in blood. His eyes were closed and he did not move.

Then Joe heard the noise. A helicopter. It was high above the broken bridge.

'A helicopter!' Joe shouted. 'Leon, look!' But Leon's eyes were closed and he said nothing.

The helicopter was soon over the rock. A rope was lowered and Joe held it. Then he tied it round Leon. Joe held Leon with one hand and he held the rope with the other. Slowly, the two men were lifted in the air.

Leon woke up slowly. He was still half-asleep.

'Where am I?' he asked.

Then he remembered the rock. And the helicopter. And Joe.

'Joe!' he shouted out. 'Where's Joe?'

'Don't worry,' said a voice. 'I'm not dead yet!'

Leon opened his eyes fully and saw Joe. Joe was smiling. Pedro and Manuel were standing next to him.

The four men were in a hut at base. Leon was lying in bed and his arm was in plaster.

'You'll feel better in a few days, Leon,' said Joe.

'I feel better now!' said Leon. 'But I need a drink.'

'Water?' asked Manuel.

'No, not water,' replied Leon. 'I don't want to see water again — not for a long time!'

And they all laughed.

Exercises

The Clearing

Label each of the items in the picture with words from the box.

trees   stove   boots   mug   tent   hat   clouds   coffee

Making Sentences

Write questions for the answers.

1 *What is Leon wearing?*
....
Leon is wearing a hat.

2 *What*
....
Manuel is wearing a head band.

3 *Where*
....
They are in a rainforest.

4 *What*
....
They are looking at rain clouds.

5 *Why*
....
They are looking at rain clouds because it is going to rain.

6 *Why*
....
They are wearing boots because the ground is wet.

7 *Are*
....
No, there are no roads in the rainforest.

8 *What*
....
Manuel is making coffee.

9 *Who*
....
They are waiting for Joe and Pedro.

10 *What*
....
They are going to return to their base.

Story Outline

Complete the gaps. Use each word in the box once.

called	leave	men	speak	camp	kilometres	roads
journey	again	live	tents	return	metals	away	jeep
mud	cross	without	late	houses	heavy	ago	ground
wet	waiting	down	already	names	them	forest

There are four [1]...... *men* ...... in the rainforest. Their [2]...........................
are Leon, Manuel, Pedro and Joe. Three of [3].......................................
are Brazilian. Joe is American. They [4]..
Portuguese and English.

There are no villages in the [5].. . People do
not [6].................................... here. The men are living in
[7]... for a few days. They have come from their
base [8].. . The base camp is fifty
[9].................................... away. It has wooden [10].................................... .
It does not have tents.

There are no [11].. leading back to the base.
The ground is [12].. . It has rained
[13].................................... and it is going to rain [14].................................... .
This time of year is [15].. the Rainy Season.
There is [16].. rain every year at this time.
The [17].. will get wetter. The tracks through
the forest will turn to [18]................................ .

The [19].. back to base camp will be
difficult and dangerous. The men will have to [20]....................................
a wide stream.

34

Why are these men in the forest? They are looking for
21... . There are rocks in the forest that contain
metal. Joe and Pedro left the camp two days 22................................. .
They drove 23... in a jeep. Now Leon and
Manuel are 24.. for them. When Joe and
Pedro 25..., they will all go back to base.
They will go in the 26.. .

Leon wants to take 27............................... the tents. He wants to
28.................................... before the rain starts. But he cannot leave
29... the jeep. He is angry. Where is Joe? Why
is Joe 30.......................................?

Multiple Choice

Tick the best answer.

1 What languages do the men speak?
a ☐ French and Portuguese.
b ☐ Spanish and English.
c ☐ Spanish and Portuguese.
d ☑ Portuguese and English.

2 Why are the men in the rainforest?
a ☐ They are camping in tents.
b ☐ They are looking for metal.
c ☐ They are hunting animals.
d ☐ They want to cut down trees.

3 There are no roads in the forest, but there are ...
a ☐ tracks.
b ☐ treks.
c ☐ trucks.
d ☐ tricks.

4 How many people live in the rainforest?
a ☐ A few people.
b ☐ No one.

35

c ☐ A lot of people.
d ☐ Not many people.

5 Leon wants to take down the tents. What is the opposite of
take down?
a ☐ Take off.
b ☐ Put off.
c ☐ Take up.
d ☐ Put up.

6 How far is it to base camp?
a ☐ 5 hours.
b ☐ 50 kilometres.
c ☐ 5000 meters.
d ☐ 50 miles.

7 Why is the ground wet?
a ☐ It is going to rain.
b ☐ They are near a river.
c ☐ The Rainy Season is coming.
d ☐ It has rained already.

8 What do you think is the opposite of *Rainy Season?*
a ☐ Wet Season.
b ☐ Humid Season.
c ☐ Sunny Season.
d ☐ Dry Season.

9 What is mud?
a ☐ Earth and water.
b ☐ Hard ground.
c ☐ Grassland.
d ☐ Soft rocks.

10 What is another word for *dangerous?*
a ☐ Unsafe.
b ☐ Secure.
c ☐ Wild.
d ☐ Difficult.

11 What is another word for *journey*?

a ☐ Diary.

b ☐ Journal.

c ☐ Crossing.

d ☐ Trip.

12 How will the men travel back to base camp?

a ☐ By helicopter.

b ☐ By bus.

c ☐ On foot.

d ☐ By jeep.

13 Why is Leon angry?

a ☐ Joe and Pedro have not returned.

b ☐ Manuel has not taken down the tents.

c ☐ Manuel has not finished making the coffee.

d ☐ He has seen rain clouds in the sky.

Grammar Focus: *Present Perfect Tense*

Answer the questions using the Present Perfect tense and the prompts.

1 Why is the ground wet?
(it/rain) ....*Because it has rained.*..

2 Why is Leon angry?
(Joe and Pedro/not return) ....

3 Why can't they see the sun?
(clouds/cover sky) ....

4 Why are the tents still standing?
(Manuel/not take down) ....

5 How do they know that rain is coming?
(they/see clouds) ....

6 Where have Joe and Pedro been?
(they/be out in the forest) ....

Words From the Story 1

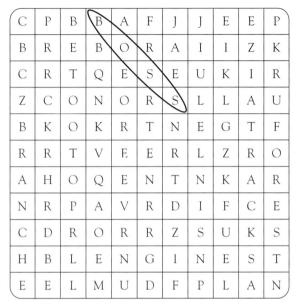

C	P	B	B	A	F	J	J	E	E	P
B	R	E	B	O	R	A	I	I	Z	K
C	R	T	Q	E	S	E	U	K	I	R
Z	C	O	N	O	R	S	L	L	A	U
B	K	O	K	R	T	N	E	G	T	F
R	R	T	V	E	E	R	L	Z	R	O
A	H	O	Q	E	N	T	N	K	A	R
N	R	P	A	V	R	D	I	F	C	E
C	D	R	O	R	R	Z	S	U	K	S
H	B	L	E	N	G	I	N	E	S	T
E	E	L	M	U	D	F	P	L	A	N

Find words in the square with the meanings below. The numbers in brackets show the number of letters in each word.

1 Person in charge (4) .... *BOSS* ....
2 Part of a tree that grows from the trunk (6) ....
3 Not in one piece or not working (6) ....
4 To be all over something (5) ....
5 The machine that makes a car etc move (6) ....
6 Responsibility for a mistake (5) ....
7 A place with a lot of trees (6) ....
8 A 4x4 vehicle (4) ....
9 Soft earth and water (3) ....
10 Something that you have decided to do (4) ....
11 The loud noise of a lion or an engine (4) ....
12 Rough paths – not roads (6) ....

Words From the Story 2

Unjumble the letters to make words that complete the sentences.

1 SOBS   Leon is in charge. He's the .... *boss* ....

2 CHARBN   Leon's arm was broken by a tree ....

3 NOKERB   They cannot drive across the river because the

bridge is ....

4 CEDROVE   Driving is difficult because the tracks are

.... with mud.

5 CHOPRELITE   Base camp sends a ....
to rescue them.

6 NIGENE   Their jeep is powerful. It has a 4-litre

....

7 LAFUT   The rain has started. They left their camp too

late. Leon says it is all Joe's ....

8 LANP   'I know how to cross the river,' said Joe. 'I have a

....'

9 LEDPAD   Two men .... the
rubber boat across the river.

10 RELAWALFT   Joe and Leon are stuck on a rock in the river.

The rock is above a ....

11 OPER   They tie the boat to the bridge with ....

Published by Macmillan Education
Between Towns Road, Oxford OX4 3PP
Macmillan Education is an imprint of
Macmillan Publishers Limited
Companies and representatives throughout the world

ISBN 978 0 2300 3503 4
ISBN 978 1 4050 7612 8 (with CD pack)

Illustrated by Donald Harley
Original cover template design by Jackie Hill
Cover photography by Image Bank

Printed in Thailand
2010 2009 2008
5 4 3 2 1

with CD pack
2010 2009 2008
10 9 8 7 6